Step Into Your Value

Step Into Your Value

Erica Quigley

Some details have been changed to protect individuals' anonymity. These are my memories, from my perspective, and I have tried to represent events as faithfully as possible. Some sample scenarios in this book are fictitious. Any similarity to actual persons, living or dead, is coincidental.

To everyone who desires to live the life of their dreams.
And to Charlotte and Reagan, who gave me the deeper reason to desire mine.

Table of Contents

Prologue i

Introduction 1

Part 1: Foundation 5

   Your Perspective 9

   What is Value? 12

   4 Non-Negotiable Pillars 13

   Self-Sabotage and Imposter Syndrome 16

   The Change Curve and Impact of Instant Decisions....18

   The Heart and The Head 20

   Foundations Summary 24

   Foundations Reflection 25

Part 2: The Heart...27

   External Validation 30

   Internal Validation 31

   How to Build Internal Validation.............................33

   Identity..34

   Environment..39

   The Heart Summary 42

   The Heart Reflection 43

Part 3: The Head 45

   Time Value 48

   Step 1: Start with the End in Mind...........................49

   Step 2: Your Work Week..51

Step 3: Your Work Year 53

Step 4: Your Target Per Hour 55

Now What? 56

Transitioning From Hourly to Project or Retainer.............................. 57

The Head Summary.. 59

The Head Reflection 60

Wrap Up **61**

Resources and Inspiration **62**

Prologue

Sitting on the 14th floor of a glitzy highrise overlooking Philadelphia, the room was spinning so fast I couldn't even begin to concentrate on the job candidate I was interviewing. Under the table, I pushed my fingers up against the metal to steady myself, thinking over and over again, "You're in one spot. You're not moving."

I tried listening to what the man was saying, doing my best to pretend nothing was wrong. *You're fine, Erica. You're sitting still.* I felt so dizzy and lightheaded and nauseous and the room kept spinning and spinning.

The interview was with a candidate to replace my boss. Putting in over 100 hours a week I'd found rapid success in my career, and had accumulated a long list of responsibilities that was equally as impressive.

By 30, my salary had hit six figures. I was now 34 and on track to make $175,000 that year. This was the success I visualized growing up when I watched my mom go out and find a job as a newly single parent with three daughters to support. This lit the fire in me: No matter what, earning as much money as I could became my dream. The job wasn't important. Stability and freedom (or, what I thought was freedom) were what mattered to me.

And here I was, a mother myself to two young daughters and director of the global supply chain for a technology company that provided direct services from California to the United Kingdom. From the corporate office in Philadelphia, I managed a team of employees, as well as the logistics for our proprietary software and our products across five time zones.

I wasn't sleeping — at all, practically. On any given day, I might have a meeting at 6 a.m. with sales in London and another to take an order at

10 p.m. to ship from Sacramento. If the meeting was too early or too late, I took it, to save my team from the burnout I was feeling.

But I felt no amount of hard work was ever enough. I pushed myself to do more and work more hours. I scheduled conference calls for my commute home and when I got there, I ate a quick dinner with my husband and children and then worked all night at my computer in the basement.

Here's the twisted logic that set the room spinning during the interview that day in 2018 and put me in the hospital: I followed advice I'd found online about how to survive on as little sleep as possible. While nursing, I got in the habit of working until 3 a.m. when it was time for my youngest daughters overnight feeding. Then, I would lay down to sleep and set my alarm for 40 minutes so I wouldn't hit a REM cycle. I would get showered and dressed and in the car by 5:25 a.m., and I'd start the workday all over again.

I had such severe sleep deprivation I wasn't thinking clearly and I most definitely wasn't performing clearly at work or at home.

Sitting in the interview that day, I tried to steer the conversation to its end. I couldn't take the dizziness anymore. It felt worse than any late night in college when I'd stumbled to bed after drinking too much. This time, of course, I didn't have a thing to drink and I was scared — and not only because of my medical symptoms.

An hour earlier, I stood before my company's CFO looking out the floor-to-ceiling windows in his office and I gave him my notice. He knew how much I was working, and he knew I wasn't happy.

I didn't have another job lined up. Instead, I'd long promised myself I would take the leap of faith and start my own company. It's something I wanted to do since high school when I won a top prize from the National Foundation for Teaching Entrepreneurship and a trip to New York City to present my business plan for the custom-made clothing company I'd conceived. I'd put myself through Virginia Tech after high school and earned a bachelor's of science degree. After graduation, though, my focus became paying off student loans, earning money and getting promoted.

Now, after about a decade, I'd found the stability I wanted and I was ready to create the freedom I yearned for…

The vertigo had been on and off for months. On that particular day my dizziness came on when I was talking to the CFO earlier, and by the time I'd ended the candidate's interview I had to find my coworker I'd carpooled with to tell her I needed to get home. I felt awful.

That night, I tried to sleep away my symptoms, but they were even worse by morning. I couldn't sit up, reading my phone was impossible and I was throwing up. I called my sister to take me to the emergency room so my husband could stay home with our daughters.

I was admitted to the hospital and told I might be having a stroke. By this point, I could barely talk. Through testing over several days, my medical team eventually determined I was experiencing severe vertigo brought on by stress and extreme sleep deprivation.

It took five days in the hospital to get my condition manageable. Even after I was discharged, I needed to use a walker and I relied on a home health aide to help teach me how to walk with my symptoms. I didn't recover for five months.

This experience, as you might expect, was a wake-up call for me. I understood the consequences of my drive to achieve more and more and more. I had put myself in a dangerous situation. But I thought that was the way to success. I was sacrificing my time and my health — myself — to give my family a good life. I now knew this wasn't the right answer.

Even so, resting and recuperating did not come easy. My youngest daughter had just turned one and my eldest was almost three. My husband was a stay-at-home dad, so my paycheck had been our only income and, oh yeah, I had just resigned from my job.

To get through this difficult period, I did a lot of reflecting. I listened to podcasts and tried to soak up all the advice and inspiration I could find from entrepreneurs and business experts, and began networking. I began to work with various mentors and I tapped into an entire network filled with people like me who believed in their ability to run their own businesses, create an income and find success and fulfillment on their own terms.

Here's what I learned: The traditional dogma that has you believe you always have to work harder and harder and work more hours to earn money just isn't true. In those first few months I found proof there are people making real money not based on the hours they work or the number of 'widgets' they produce.

I said to myself, this was the point at which I had to decide if I was going to put all I could into creating a path to make the money I wanted while living the lifestyle I wanted. I made a promise that I would never again work myself into the hospital.

For years, I knew I wanted to run my own business. This isn't unusual. Lots of people have similar dreams and goals, but only a small percentage actually believe what they want is possible. An even smaller percentage pursue the possibilities.

While I long believed running my own business was possible (I learned that in high school), I still had to understand what held me back for all of those years. I worked around the clock, all the while wishing things would have been different. I defined my value by the support I provided to others — my employer, the team members I managed and, of course, my husband and children. What I wanted felt like too high of a burden. Ultimately, I feared starting my own company would risk the financial stability my family had become accustomed to.

Through this reflection I was able to unlock transformational thinking: I had to stop trading time for money. I took my background in business operations and figured out how to use that knowledge to give companies my outsider's perspective and lead them to greater success. And, I realized this wasn't just true for myself but also for my clients and the entrepreneurs around me. **People needed to learn time wasn't their value, it was knowledge.**

I've observed clients now at different levels and stages of business but all faced a consistent pattern. No matter their age, gender or company size, they de-valued themselves. It was the same experience for my client who was a new freelance artist as it was for the established wholesale market owner who inherited the business from his father as it was for the doctor with multiple practices. They all believed their time was worth less than it actually was.

This observation opened my eyes, and I started seeing this pattern in all types of life — people in corporate America, the gig economy and consulting firms. I saw it in stay-at-home parents and college students. It struck me: so many people don't believe in their dreams, or their ability to become a future version of themselves.

But their value — your value — is there. Each one of us has it.

In the years since I started my own business I have written an award-winning book called "Business Process Flow Mapping Succinctly," which was purchased and published by the global software company SyncFusion. My girls are now ages 6 and 8. My company is now a team of people who support me, and at this point in time have served over 42 growing companies.

My work is a flexible 25 hour week and I'm more highly compensated than I was at the technology company. I am the same person. The difference is I opened my mind to new and diverse ideas and I was brave enough to step into my value. And, through reading this book, I'm confident you'll step into yours.

Through my guided lessons, we'll explore ideas and tactics to allow you to emotionally and logically step into your true value. Let's go.

Introduction

ERICA QUIGLEY

When reading, there may be ideas you've been exposed to before, and others, you have not. To that end, while reading (and honestly this is a great exercise to apply in all aspects of your life), approach the concepts with the perspective that:

1. There are things you know.
2. There are things you know you don't know.
3. There are things you don't know that you don't know.

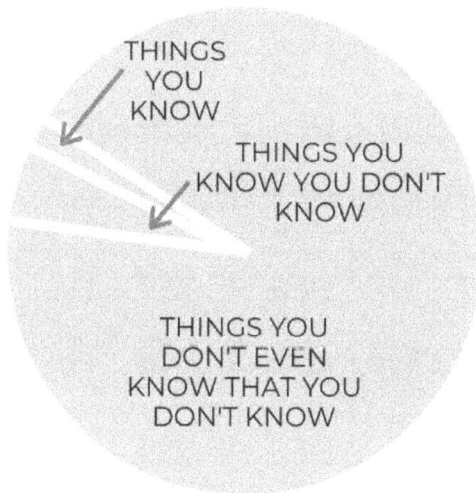

If applying these ideas is a new perspective for you, it may be helpful to imagine you have a set of glasses to put on which allow you to view from this perspective. The lenses allow you to zoom outside of your current vision and see the extent of the great unknown as it relates to your current known. The relationship between these two lenses or perspectives can actually change your knowledge.

The best way to process through these perspectives is to follow along with the exercises and spend time thinking and feeling into the answers. If you do this very important work, it will be that much easier to take the leaps within, allowing you to step into your true value.

Part 1: Foundation

ERICA QUIGLEY

February 5, 2020

Good morning--

Here you are, on the verge of becoming the next level of you.

So keep on going then.

GET UP.

You've done harder things than today

Get up and do the thing that will make you great

This is your life. This is your day. Do the things you need to do to make yourself the person you want to be.

These things ...are who you are.

These things... are who you are meant to be.

On this journey we're going to stop being our biggest critic. Instead, we'll walk through the steps to **continually elevate the way you perceive yourself**.

We have the power to control our perception. And we can elevate or devalue ourselves with that power.

Did you ever hear the story about Jim Carey when he played as Andy Kaufman in Man on the Moon? He wanted to encompass the character of Andy so deeply, he approached it with Method Acting– to totally take on the characteristics of Andy both on and off screen. He essentially wired his brain to believe he was Andy. And when filming concluded he had to bring himself back to who he really was.

We can use our brain as a powerful tool.

In fact, most of our lives we have likely wired our brains to devalue ourselves. So here in the Foundation is where we acknowledge that– and then prove to ourselves that we can fix it. And that is the basis of how we will step into our true and inherent value and worth.

The idea that we have been devaluing ourselves most of our lives may be a sobering realization. And the idea that we are essentially going to **think bigger** of ourselves may have triggered some. So let's take a hot minute to process this sentence...

We're going to walk through the steps to **continually elevate the way you perceive yourself**.

When we think about perceiving ourselves a certain way, the first thing that may strike us is ego.

Who are we to think about ourselves in a bigger way? I don't want to be someone who "fakes it".

...But, you can think more of yourself and not be fake. You can love yourself, value your time, your dreams and your ideas.

After all, if not you then who?

Do you want to be a victim to your perception or do you want to be empowered by it? **We have the ability to do either. Let's choose wisely.**

Your perspective

Everyone is living in their own reality with their own unique set of circumstances which shape their perspectives. Your interpretation of your value and contribution to the world depends on your perspective. You may physically see yourself, but have thoughts or feelings that cause you to see yourself in a different way.

I've caught myself thinking I'm not smart enough or I don't have the right qualifications. But, is that really true? And who actually sets that standard?

Someone on my team recently sent me information about an award she wanted me to apply for. I almost disregarded it, thinking I wasn't "ready" for it. And then I realized, what if I could see myself the way she sees me?

She obviously sees me as someone who should be receiving this award. What if I could give myself the same perspective?

On the following page is an exercise in how you view yourself. Take a few minutes to jot down your thoughts.

At the end of this chapter we'll go through this exercise again-- but we'll work through exactly who it is you **want** to see when you look at yourself.

YOUR INTERPRETATION
DEPENDS ON YOUR
PERSPECTIVE

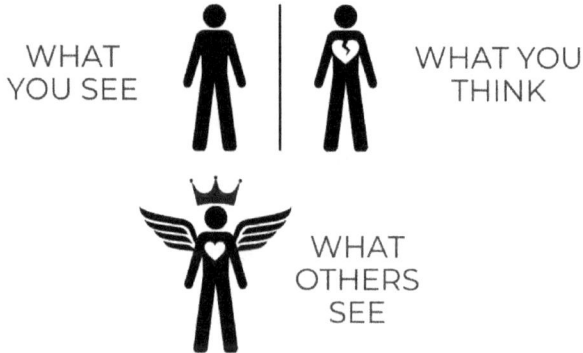

WHAT
YOU SEE

WHAT YOU
THINK

WHAT
OTHERS
SEE

EXERCISE
Imagine you are looking at yourself from the third person. What do you see? Are you looking down, up or straight at yourself? What's your expression? What's your stance? Do you appear confident or insecure? What are you wearing? Where are you? Are you doing anything? Arguably, the most important and life changing thing you can do for yourself is choose to see yourself in a different way, from a different lens. Once you begin to see yourself in this new way, you can begin to act in accordance with what you see.

What is value?

What does it mean to you? Worth, importance, a monetary price tag?

The trickiness of how this word can describe both one's personal objectives in life and money in your wallet can contribute to our feelings of money equaling value.

Then, if our minds have associated the two together, when we feel like we "don't have enough money" for something it contributes to us not feeling like we are important or worthy, i.e. "enough". It's a perpetual cycle that some can be stuck in for their entire lives.

However, we can reassociate this in a more positive, expansive way.

Money is neutral. It does not decide to accumulate for only certain people.

Instead of letting money be the driver of our feelings of value, we can let our feelings of value be the driver of the money we make.

This very slight change means that as long as we make the decision to have money, then we will have it.

We don't think that because we haven't had money up to this point that we must not be able to have more. We instead change our mind and decide that now is the time we will have money.

Reassociating value to mean— **the more we believe in and find ourselves worthy then the more money we will earn— will allow us to continually step into more impactful work and activities.**

VALUE
Value can be associated with the internal feelings of yourself. It can also be associated with money or external assessment. And so value is a tricky word. And it can feel tricky to want to "step into" it. In this text, value means the way you feel about yourself. And also, in order to value your time and therefore value yourself, we will associate money with value too.

4 Non-Negotiable Pillars

To step into your value and continually rise, there's a few pillars to cover. We must approach elevating our value with these four beliefs or pillars as our foundation.

1. There is inherent good and abundance in the world.
2. You are whole and worthy to hold (and then expand) your space.
3. The value you place upon yourself is simply your perception of how you relate to the world right now.
4. You can instantly change the value you place upon yourself (This can happen in either direction. It can also take someone an entire lifetime to believe they can change their value. Our goal here is to allow you the proof to believe it instantly.)

There is Inherent Good and Abundance in the World

The world is full and abundant of what you want. The greater good is here to support you. Trust and lean into the possibilities. Instead of *worrying* about what might happen, reframe into being *excited* about what might happen.

As children we are excited about what the world and future holds, but as we grow up we begin to assess risk. Instead of being excited, we learn to tamper those feelings to avoid disappointment. We do this because we aren't trusting and leaning into the good in the world.

You Are Whole and Worthy to Hold (And Then Expand) Your Space

There are people who dream, but their brain can't logically understand how the inherent good and abundance in the world could support them, and therefore they dismiss their dreams as fantasy.

You were not born into the world by accident and you don't have dreams by accident. Whatever is in your heart is the reason you are here. And searching for or experimenting with the reason is also completely valid.

The Value You Place Upon Yourself is Simply Your Perception of How You Relate to the World Right Now

However you pictured yourself in the previous exercise is based upon how you relate to yourself right now. Up until today you have lived in a somewhat fixed or slowly elevating self-perception. Your current self-perception may even have been entirely based on externalities (which we will cover in the next part). Your life, the people, and the events within it have caused you to have your own beliefs and value, and it has also evolved into giving you the current perception of yourself.

You Can Instantly Change the Value You Place Upon Yourself

It is simply a decision. But some decisions can be tricky. If everyone understood they could instantly change their self-perception-- and, in turn, their value, the world would be a different place. Whether you believe this yet or not is up to you, but the text within will help you accept and apply the concept.

One note though... Be aware that you can move your self value in either direction. For example, if you find yourself with people who deplete your energy or in a run down environment you will notice your self value may diminish. Intentionally monitoring and utilizing your environment and reinforcing your personal value through external circumstances are extremely helpful ways to keep yourself aligned. The best way to contradict an experience that diminishes your sense of internal value is to acknowledge what is happening and apply the exercises throughout this book to elevate yourself instead.

....

If you are looking for more work and integration I highly recommend digging into the resources I've listed at *www.stepintoyourvalue.com*

Self-Sabotage and Imposter Syndrome

In my work, I've come across clients who have had a mix of beliefs which caused them at various times to both elevate and devalue themselves. At first, I didn't understand why they struggled. These people were all smart and completely competent, yet the actions I observed did not make any logical sense to me. It would become clear though, after a few weeks with each of these clients, they were taking actions to sabotage themselves.

After I observed this self-sabotage phenomenon with several clients in varying circumstances and industries I became fascinated with the idea of personal value and personal perception.

There was a doctor, who even after years of having his practices (three locations), was still operating all 3 businesses out of his personal bank account. Not only was it a tax nightmare, but he had no idea if he was profitable or what he could afford to do. Even when we set him up with a bookkeeper who was experienced at sorting out these situations, the doctor deprioritized answering the bookkeeper's phone calls or emails and therefore did not get himself out of his situation.

There was an artist who would do online business development, book projects and contracts. She would do all the work to create the art. But then she would let it sit, not answer clients, and then not deliver the finished product on time even though they were ready.

There was a CEO of a 100+ person operation who would not hold anyone, not even his direct reports, accountable for the work they were supposed to be doing. He would let Directors in his company take advantage of the flexible work environment. He would let them provide the same status updates at meetings for weeks on end. And no matter how unhappy he was with anyone's performance (or lack thereof) he didn't put anyone on a performance plan or replace anyone. Instead he let them drag along with the company for months or even years until they quit.

These are just a few of the countless examples I observed and it didn't seem to matter the industry, the position, the size, or the age of the company. They all had a common thread.

Their self-sabotaging behavior was due to a lack of belief in themselves. They didn't believe they were "valuable enough to succeed". In fact, they also didn't even believe they could change their own circumstances. Instead, they were operating in victim mode and wanted someone to save them.

Most times, they would exhibit self-sabotaging behaviors over and over and over again. And it would perpetuate the idea that they shouldn't believe in themselves. And then therefore they continued to feel stuck.

I realized they were fulfilling what they believed themselves to be. If they were to be "successful" and "happy" they would feel like they were an imposter because they didn't feel they deserved it. So they would do things like not return emails, not respond to clients, and not enforce rules with staff to keep themselves "unsuccessful" so they would never have to come upon feeling like they were an imposter.

Their limiting beliefs kept them from being wildly successful in their business, and also caused them conflict in their personal lives.

The Change Curve and Impact of Instant Decisions

I think there are many different reasons, or root causes, why we can question ourselves and our value. In my work and with the clients I previously mentioned, I observed it as making simple business mistakes and even though they had all the resources to fix them, they allowed the mistakes to set the stage for not trusting themselves. Then when they didn't trust themselves they could justify they could never step into their true value and become their version of success.

When I'm working with companies on their business process, we usually refer to the Kubler-Ross Change Curve[1]. In psychology this curve shows how we as humans move through change. When we are presented with change we experience different feelings, which then allow us to move through the change.

As it relates to placing value upon ourselves in order to achieve what we want, I'd apply the same logic here.

For those who can't reconcile what they want (their true desire) with who they are (their perception), they are likely to stay stuck and possibly even ping pong between Frustration, Depression, and Experiment.

After all, personal value can be so intangible.

---

[1] https://www.ekrfoundation.org/5-stages-of-grief/change-curve/

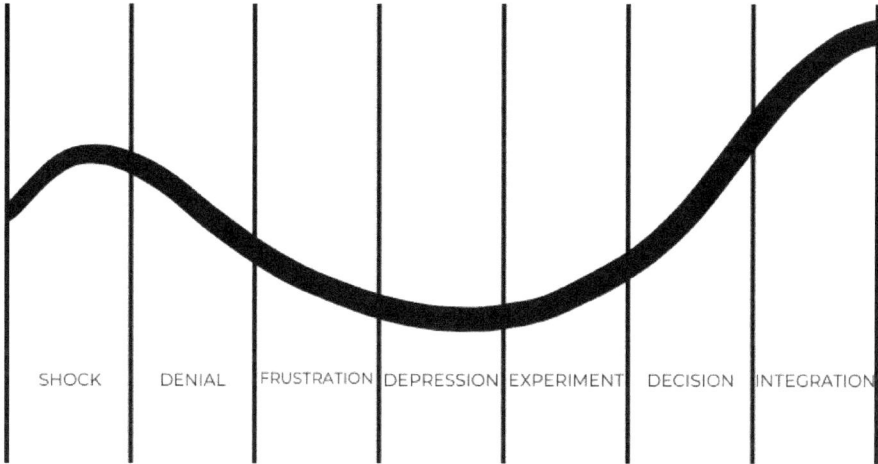

| SHOCK | DENIAL | FRUSTRATION | DEPRESSION | EXPERIMENT | DECISION | INTEGRATION |

Figure 1: The Kubler-Ross Change Curve

I realized that those who are "stuck" (but may not even realize they are stuck) may need to apply something tangible to their personal value. Relating the tangible to value allows your brain to apply logic in order to move us through to the Decision on the Change Curve to accept our value.

As a contrast to my self-sabotaging clients, I have also had the pleasure of working with clients who believed in their own potential.

The difference is they made a decision to believe in themselves. They made a decision to step into the future version of themselves they wanted to be. They know all success also comes with failures. They don't let the failures define them. They take the lessons and keep moving forward.

Think about it like this:

We make thousands of decisions every day. Some are instant, some we mull over for hours or possibly days. What if the decision to elevate your personal value was an instant one? It can be. You can decide today-- right now-- to begin living as the person you want to be.

The quicker this logic is applied, the faster and more instantly the change and the step into your desired value can occur.

The Heart and the Head

From my vantage point, my brain tends to support all ideas with logic. I know now that's part of my upbringing and personality type, and is probably why I was drawn to and therefore trained in business process and efficiency. I have very technical skills. For most of my years I led my life with the thought that we as humans are simply lemmings meant as a collective for something larger and there was no use trying to emotionally grow. It's taken me years of reading, learning, exploring, to come to "terms" with the idea that I'm presenting in this text.

That said– do I have a process for stepping into your value? Yes. For those of us who aren't lucky enough to possess the magic of instant decision making, I have a very detailed step-by-step plan to allow your brain to accept the decision to do it. But, what I have noticed is there are two pieces.

The brain will not allow yourself to complete the steps if your Heart does not believe and trust in what you are doing. And conversely the Heart does not allow you to dream incrementally bigger and bigger if the Brain has no idea what steps it might take to achieve.

And for that reason, the upcoming sections of the book are broken into Heart and Head.

Without laying the foundation of the Heart, the pieces in your Head can be implemented-- BUT if they are challenged they can easily crumble. And if that happens-- your Head will most likely not allow yourself to try to implement again, or it will keep you on a small scale-- because you have found reasons why "stepping into your value" doesn't work for you.

If you think back to the Kubler Ross Change Curve, this is what causes someone to bounce between the stages before Decision.

If you believe your Heart is in it, but you have these small nagging pieces of your brain that allow your Heart to question if you are allowed to hold your value, the Head will address the logical reconciliation for your Heart which should then allow you to *decide*.

Although there is a bit of tapping into the free spirit here when it comes to The Heart, we can approach even this with structure and logic (if it's helpful- some of you will not need that).

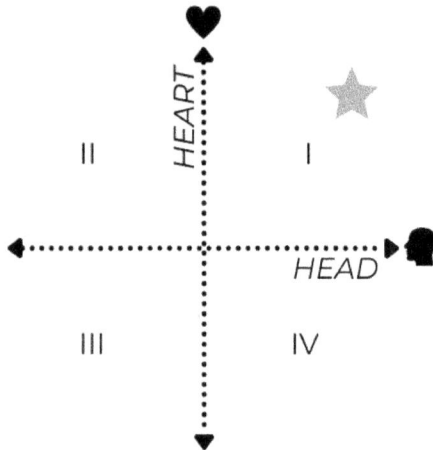

Instead of aiming for Quadrant IV (as pictured above, which would be just teaching you the tactics and the step-by-step) we are aiming for an unshakeable belief which will allow you to *continue* to step into a higher and higher personal value, as illustrated by the star in Quadrant I.

In different terms, if the feelings and beliefs of The Heart and the logic and the tactics of The Head overlapped into a Venn diagram, the intersection of those would sculpt the ideal personal identity.

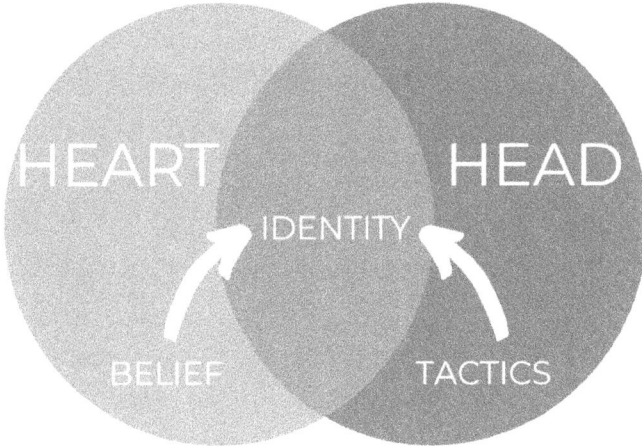

With this foundation laid, my goal for you with the remainder of this text is to be able to understand the fundamentals of what you can put in place to get you to Quadrant I, and to continue to elevate yourself into whatever identity you desire, for the rest of your life.

Foundations Summary:

1. There are things you know, things you know you don't know, and things you don't know you don't know. Embrace life with this understanding.

2. You have the ability to instantly change your perspective.

3. The world will support you in your journey but you must allow it.

4. Recognize when you are making a decision to sabotage your success so you can decide to step into your value instead.

5. Allowing both your heart and your head to step into your value will give you the foundation of unshakeable confidence.

Foundations Reflection:

Now that the foundation is laid, it's time to put your ideas to paper. Grab a journal to answer the following questions so you can solidify this in your mind.

Imagine you are looking at yourself from the third person. What do you want to see? Who do you want to be?

Are you looking down, up or straight at yourself? What's your expression? What's your stance? Do you appear confident? What are you wearing? Where are you? Are you doing anything?

Take a breath. You have permission now to step into and be this person.

ERICA QUIGLEY

Part 2: The Heart

ERICA QUIGLEY

January 9, 2021

In every great story, there's a vision & there's a transformation...
Because the vision requires us to become next level to achieve it.

One year ago this week I became Erica 3.0. I can specifically recall going
from 1.0 to 2.0. And I can still feel going from 2.0 to 3.0.
The emotions. The feelings. The actions.

For the last few weeks I've been struggling. I have a force, it's pulling me
towards Erica 4.0. I've been scared. I've been resisting. And it's funny...
because I've been trying to become 4.0 since the day I transformed to 3.0.
I could see it. I could visualize it. But I was trying to push myself towards
it. It didn't feel easy.

And I've noticed, whenever something feels difficult, something is not
quite right. Something needs to be aligned. Imagine trying to force
yourself to run up a hill to the top, but the top is a mirage. You don't get
there. You're treadmilling. In the same spot.

But then something clicks. You shift your gaze a bit,
You realize.. it's right there. Just step off the treadmill and take one jump
forward. Then reach out and grab it.

I felt the shift this week. I'm not pushing any longer. I'm being pulled.

We kid ourselves. We think it has to be harder than it is. We think it's
uphill.

What if what you wanted, Was right here, Pulling you towards it?

There are different strategies we employ to believe in ourselves.

External Validation

You can believe in yourself because you see proof or results. Maybe someone reaches out to tell you they admire what you are doing. Or perhaps you receive an email response which says "good job". This is an external validation. From personal experience, this can work, but you can't control how sustainable this is. And, if the external validation disappears it can set you up for a rude awakening if you don't also have an internal validation.

For example, take Lucy, a business owner who thrives off of the responses she receives from her clients. They praise her for answering emails late at night and on weekends. They say things like " thanks for all of your hard work!"

While it seems like there's no harm in those types of praise, even when she receives a comment like "this is awesome", or "great work" she unfortunately relates it to her constant grinding. She's begun to value herself based upon the external validation received from her clients. Her belief that she is valuable is linked to her "hard work" and has proven to her (in her brain) that working hard = income = value.

Lucy believes in her own ability to work hard because that is what she knows. Therefore she trusts her income is there for her and she feels valuable, because she will "always" be a hard worker. She even describes herself as such.

BUT if you remove the hard work or the income, Lucy's identity begins to crumble.

Let's say Lucy hires herself a rockstar employee. This person notices how much Lucy is working and tries to help by picking up where she can. Lucy is likely to fill the gap with other "hard work" and just keep piling it on, or she's likely to find it very difficult to let go and delegate. She may micromanage everything. She may feel like it would be done better if she just did it herself.

So what is the phenomenon which keeps Lucy entangled with wanting to do "hard work" and work long hours?

Remember that for Lucy, hard work = income = value. If the "hard work" was removed, even if her income remains the same, she begins to feel not as worthy or as valuable. She feels like she hasn't earned the income and does not feel personal value.

While external validation is nice, it can't be someone's sole source of feeling value.

Internal Validation

On the other hand (and hopefully in addition to external validation), you can believe in yourself *simply because*. Simply because there is inherent good in the world. Simply because you are whole and worthy just as you are.

You can internally know you are valid and valued for simply the reason that you are. No immediate or external proof required. Some of the strongest coaches and leaders share examples of when their internal validation is tested, for example, financially. And the point is, that even in what would seem to be the lowest of lows, they are OK because of their belief in themselves. I've heard examples of bankruptcy and foreclosure. No matter what difficult circumstance someone is put in, if you are internally validated then you are OK with whatever the result is because you believe in your heart you have everything you need to get through.

Internally you know that everything you need you already have. You know that everything you desire is available to you. And, you are already perfect as-is.

With this mindset, Lucy would be thrilled to hire a rockstar. She would realize what an amazing opportunity to create a larger impact she now has. She can receive help and tap deeper into her gifts. She would allow herself to welcome the income that she receives and appreciate the gift of time and what she can now do with it, even if she is physically working less hours.

Once you get to this place, you can truly harness your potential. Your internal belief will snowball and accumulate.

How to Build Internal Validation

Why do we allow externalities to impact beliefs about ourselves? Because we are searching for ways to feel valid because they do not already exist within us.

In the previous section I wrote a pretty key sentence. **Everything you need you already have.**

This may be a tough one to believe, particularly if you've been searching for external validation, if you're in the midst of rough times, or if you've never been told that before in your life.

For example, what if you're broke and on the brink of financial disaster? How can you already have everything you need?

Maybe what you *need* is a steady stream of income and to get on top of your bills.

Within yourself is the resourcefulness to find or create a steady stream of income. BUT you have to recognize it is there. You have to believe and trust in yourself. You have to believe you contain the resourcefulness.

That part can be tough to crack, especially if you're in a down spot.

So how do we build internal validation? How do we believe everything we need we already have? How do we learn to trust in ourselves?

We need to create a positive self identity and an environment that fosters it.

Identity

Your identity, as defined here, is the way you view yourself and who you believe you currently are, and who you are not. This is composed of and reflected in, the words you speak, the actions you take, and the way you present yourself.

If you believe you are not worthy of living in peace then you will not live in peace. You will surround yourself with news articles that prove the opposite. Your social media feeds will perpetuate it. You'll allow toxic people into your space.

If you believe you are not worthy of paying yourself $150,000 per year, then you will find ways to either not grow your business or have too many expenses to pay yourself $150,000 per year (by the way, the same thing can be said about $20,000 per year or $1,000,000 per year... it comes down to your belief in your worthiness to accept it).

If you believe you are not worthy of having a loving relationship, then you will not have a loving relationship. You will be too busy, you will settle, or you will find fault with your current partner.

If you believe that you are not worthy of being a CEO of a multi-million dollar company then you will not be a CEO of a multi-million dollar company. Your business will falter. You won't think through the growth and end up calling it quits instead of working through the frustrations into success.

The fastest path to achieving what you want is accepting the identity you want and acting in your desired identity right now. Like <u>RIGHT NOW</u>!!

That means acting like the person you desire to be (the person you wrote about in the last section).

Of course, if people were able to absorb this statement and ALLOW themselves to do this, this would be a very short book. You can know things in your heart and deeply desire them but not allow yourself to walk upon the basic stepping stones to get there.

You may *want* to live in peace, but allow yourself to keep a toxic employee on board.

You may *want* to pay yourself $150,000 per year, but continue to pay for external help as if you're seeking a silver bullet.

You may *want* to have a loving relationship, but not want to have the conflict of ending your current unfulfilled one.

You may *want* to be the CEO of a multi-million dollar company, but not reconcile your books to even know if you are profitable which will make you want to call it quits.

To reframe, you can instead lead with your Heart to know what you desire. And then act upon the tactics in your head. It makes it very transparent.

Break your sticking points into the following categories to allow your Heart and Head to align:

1. Your desire
2. Your problem which takes you away from what you desire.
3. What your problem causes.
4. What you need to do to fix it.
5. Why you will do it, which reinforces your desire.

Here's a few examples:

> *I want to live in peace* [your desire]*, but I allow myself to keep toxic employees onboard* [your problem which takes you away from your desire]*. The toxicity is in my space and affects myself, and others I care about, every day* [what your problem causes]*. I am in charge. I need to coach them up or fire them* [what you need to do to fix it]*. I choose to only perpetuate healthy workplaces* [why you will do it, which reinforces your desire].

> *I want to pay myself $150,000 per year* [your desire]*, but I'm spending revenue on other items instead of prioritizing myself to make it happen* [your problem which takes you away from your desire]*. I feel stressed and resentful when I'm not able to take home what I deserve from my business* [What your problem causes]*. I could update my business budget to focus on my pay so I don't have the funds available to spend on other areas needlessly* [what you need to do to fix it]*. When I pay myself what I desire I would be able to live comfortably and feel less stress which*

would reflect back into being a more positive leader in my business [why you will do it, which reinforces your desire]..

I want to have a loving relationship [your desire], *but I am in one now that is unfulfilling* [your problem which takes you away from your desire]. *I feel like we have grown apart and I don't have someone I can confide in anymore* [what your problem causes]. *I need to honor my feelings. We need to seek couples counseling* [what you need to do to fix it] *so our relationship can flourish* [why you will do it, which reinforces your desire].

I want to be the CEO of a multi-million dollar company [your desire], *but I don't pay attention to my numbers* [your problem which takes you away from your desire]. *I don't even know if I'm profitable* [what your problem causes]. *I need to hire someone to reconcile and run my numbers every month. I need to set specific goals for myself and the business* [what you need to do to fix it] *so I can be the CEO I desire* [why you will do it, which reinforces your desire].

If you take time to get to know the person you want to be and the next actionable steps in line with that identity, your Heart won't get tripped up and you will stay on course to step into your value.

——---------------

So here's the thing-- in order to do this you must know the person you want to be. Many times people have a rough idea or a few characteristics, but that's not usually enough to allow you to act consistently in the identity you want. You must have a clear picture of the person you wish to be.

How does this person talk?
Do they curse? Do they gossip? Are they brimming with optimism?

What do they do for fun?
Do they lounge and Netflix? Do they golf? Do they play video games?

How do they present themselves?
Are they prompt? Do they wear earrings? Do they dress comfortably?

Your identity breaks down into micro decisions throughout your day. For me, very recently, I had a sudden realization that I wasn't wearing the type of pajamas that reflected my desired identity.

It may seem silly and trivial, but when I envision who I am I do not see myself wearing sweatpants and an old paint stained college t-shirt to bed.

So I ordered a few pairs of pajamas that made me feel like a million bucks and donated the sweats I no longer needed.

Acting in your desired identity is as simple as that. If the person you want to be is someone who sits with their coffee and reads before work... then do that. You don't have to wait for a certain time and place. You don't have to think you don't deserve that now. You *do* deserve to do whatever it is you want to do. So sit with your coffee and read. If it causes a domino effect and something else can't be completed that day-- then you can either be OK with that or adjust whatever it is.

Sometimes the best way to reprioritize is to start doing the things you really want to do. And just letting whatever falls off just fall off. If it is important enough, you'll find another way to get it done, whether that is juggling responsibilities at home, asking for help, or hiring someone to take care of it.

Environment

Your environment is the sum of the places you spend your time and the items within it, and it is also the people who surround you.

Just like with your identity- there is not a right or wrong answer for your environment. It is about what makes you feel good. If going to a big box store makes you feel excited to capture a deal then good-- that's the environment for you to shop in.

But if the big box store makes you feel overwhelmed, then change the place you shop (or have someone else do the shopping).

If your office feels dark and not inspiring, then add or refresh your artwork. Add some plants. Maybe get a different office. Why allow yourself to spend your time in a place that doesn't support you?

Further, the environment or place that supports you is not just a physical location. It's also the company you keep.

We may have all heard a form of the saying from Jim Rohn that we are the average of the five people we spend the most time with. While I think this is true, there are also the spaces of social media which have the opportunity to average us down or up.

Curating who you allow into your circle is beyond the people you see or talk with. It includes the people you follow, the friends from the past who show up on Facebook, the types of ads you click on which perpetuate more targeted ads along those lines, the news articles you click on which feeds you more of that information, the YouTube videos you watch which funnel you further and further into the platform.

Imagine, instead of social media and the spaces of the internet only having the ability to pull you down, notice that they also have the power to pull you up.

Deleting Facebook can be a stretch, especially for business owners. But what if you unfollowed the community pages which were full of complaints and negativity? What if you joined Facebook groups full of inspiration and creativity and those filled your feed instead?

I'm in a Facebook group run by Denise Duffield-Thomas (author of books including Get Rich Lucky B*tch and Chillpreneur) and there are constantly wins posted. Instead of my feed being filled with complainers, I read posts celebrating how they've generated $1.5M in an hour (an actual post in the group). That's true inspiration. That's what I want to see if I'm scrolling.

You see, we don't *always* have to see it in order to believe it. But sometimes if we see things it can help us REALIZE what is actually possible. It gives us PROOF. And what better way to normalize or believe by simply changing your surroundings to mirror the person you're stepping into.

WHERE
THE
MAGIC
HAPPENS

YOUR
COMFORT
ZONE

The Heart Summary

1. You can value yourself based on externalities and internalities. Understanding both, and leveraging both, is an extremely powerful way to level up.

2. If you are lacking internal validation commit to building it up.

3. Your identity and environment are both items you can foster yourself to build internal validation.

The Heart Reflection

Do you believe in your heart of hearts that you can be and do whatever it is you want?

Is your current identity aligned with your desired identity? If not, what needs to change to get you there?

Does your current environment support your desired identity? If it doesn't, what can you change immediately to better support this journey?

ERICA QUIGLEY

Part 3: The Head

ERICA QUIGLEY

January 10, 2023

Jan 2018 I was making a New Years resolution to start my own business. I didn't know what or how.

Jan 2023 I'm celebrating that one business bringing in $492,793 in cash collected for the previous year.

Affiliate/Referral = $25,916

Consulting Projects = $58,820

Implementation Retainers/Projects = $407,147

Digital Products = $910

Boom. Let's keep on going.

Time Value

Knowing the value of your time is half the battle. Putting a tangible number on it helps your brain easily decide if something is worth your time or not.

In the book *The 4-Hour Workweek*, Tim Ferriss uses an example of scrolling through Amazon trying to find the lowest price for an item. You might save a dollar or two, but you spend an hour or more in the process. And isn't your time worth more than a dollar or two per hour?

One of the most breakthrough exercises I do with my coaching clients is help them understand the tangible monetary value of their time. The reason this is so important is not just to tell ourselves not to spend an hour trying to save a dollar on Amazon, but to understand what we should be delegating, particularly if we are trying to grow and scale a business.

—----------------

Before we get into the numbers and calculations, let's remember we are allowed to enjoy things and have fun lives. If there's something you enjoy, it doesn't matter if your time value makes sense for it. If you truly enjoy it, then that is the true value and measure. You don't have to justify what you spend your time on if you are truly in enjoyment and flow.

There is a caveat here though. If you're trying to justify spending your time on something because you're *uncomfortable* with the idea of not doing it yourself anymore than that's different. There may be things we do that are easy for us-- that is not the same as true enjoyment.

Now we are going to calculate your target dollar per hour.

> **NOTE:** You can access my online calculator at www.stepintoyourvalue.com or use the following steps

Step 1: Start With the End in Mind

We often have an idea of what we think we can earn based upon "the market". Whether that is what an annual salary would be for the type of work you do, a comparable number to what your friends earn, or what you might hear others earn.

Instead of justifying what you think you could possibly earn based upon the market and your skillset, decide on what you *actually desire* to earn.

Because we already know our mind will only allow us to follow through on achieving things that we believe we can do, I've seen this work well if you pick a low, middle, and high desired annual amount. As we do the calculations this will allow you to model different scenarios. And, as the months pass and you begin to earn the value you desire, you'll be able to easily run another set of scenarios and step into a new amount.

Of course, you could just enter $10M a year, because that's what you desire. But if your current income is $50,000 per year your mind won't be able to comprehend the jump. So you do have to pick a desired amount that feels like it could be real to you. As you continue to do this work around raising the monetary value of your time you will be able to stretch your comfort around it more and more.

In this step you are entering the annual income amount before taxes.

Your minimum desired annual amount	
Your ideal desired annual amount	
Your reach desired annual amount	

Example:

Your minimum desired annual amount	$60,000
Your ideal desired annual amount	$100,000
Your reach desired annual amount	$250,000

Step 2: Your Work Week

Now that you have determined how much money you desire to make in a year, it's time to think about the amount of time you want to spend making that money. Remember we are breaking the habit of time = money. However, as we build our businesses, we will of course spend time on it.

In this step, we are going to think about things a little differently.

Think about your ideal lifestyle. In the table below, under each day, enter the total number of hours you want to spend working.

Mon	Tue	Wed	Thur	Fri	Sat	Sun

Example:

Mon	Tue	Wed	Thur	Fri	Sat	Sun
7	7	4	7	4	0	0

Next, add up the total amount of working hours per week.

Then calculate 40% of that number and subtract it. This will give you your total "billable hours" per week.

In this calculation I'm using the term "billable" to mean the amount of hours you are working in your business that is directly related to receiving money from a client or a sale.

The reason we subtract 40% is to give us the space to spend 40% of our time on business development and administrative tasks. If you feel like you need to spend more than 40% of your time on these types of activities then feel free to use a higher percentage so you can receive a more accurate time value rate.

WEEKLY TOTAL HOURS	
MINUS 40%	-
TOTAL "BILLABLE" HOURS PER WEEK	=

Example:

WEEKLY TOTAL HOURS	*29*
MINUS 40%	*-11.60*
TOTAL "BILLABLE" HOURS PER WEEK	*=17.40*

Step 3: Your Work Year

As a business owner we may not think ahead to consider how much vacation we want to take each year. I know for myself I just like to take time when I feel I need it. But, if we are able to take a look ahead of time at how much time we want to take off each year, then we can factor that into our calculations and not let some time off affect how much we make.

TOTAL WEEKS PER YEAR	52
MINUS DESIRED VACATION WEEKS (INCLUDE HOLIDAY WEEKS IF THEY ARE GENERALLY SLOW FOR YOU)	-
EQUALS YOUR WORKING WEEKS PER YEAR	=

Example:

TOTAL WEEKS PER YEAR	*52*
MINUS DESIRED VACATION WEEKS (INCLUDE HOLIDAY WEEKS IF THEY ARE GENERALLY SLOW FOR YOU)	*- 4*
EQUALS YOUR WORKING WEEKS PER YEAR	*=48*

Now take your "total billable hours" from Step 2 and plug them into the equation below:

TOTAL BILLABLE HOURS	X TOTAL WORKING WEEKS PER YEAR	= TOTAL BILLABLE HOURS PER YEAR
	X	=

Example:

TOTAL BILLABLE HOURS	X TOTAL WORKING WEEKS PER YEAR	= TOTAL BILLABLE HOURS PER YEAR
17.40	X 48	= 835.20

Step 4: Your Target Per Hour

Take your desired annual amounts, divide them by your total billable hours per year to arrive at your low, medium and high dollar values.

	ANNUAL DESIRED INCOMES	/ TOTAL BILLABLE HOURS PER YEAR	= MONETARY VALUE PER HOUR
Minimum		/	=
Ideal		/	=
Reach		/	=

Example:

	ANNUAL DESIRED INCOMES	/ TOTAL BILLABLE HOURS PER YEAR	= MONETARY VALUE PER HOUR
Minimum	*$60,000*	*/835.20*	*=$71.84*
Ideal	*$100,000*	*/835.20*	*=$119.73*
Reach	*$250,000*	*/835.20*	*=$299.33*

Now What?

These numbers are what they are. I've seen them come back at $20/hour, $2,000/hour and everything in between.

If you are a business owner who's using your own time to provide a service, then this is a great starting point to ensure you are "selling your time" for the amount that is in line with your goal. You can use your newly discovered dollar-per-hour to adjust your package prices (if you bill hourly, then you can also check out the next section "Transitioning from hourly to project or retainer").

If you provide a service but have employees or contractors who help with fulfillment, this is a good opportunity to ensure you're not spending more time on the work than your "dollar-per-hour" calls for. If you are, then you can either adjust the amount of time you spend on client work or adjust the clients prices.

If you sell products, your dollar-per-hour can help ensure you are spending your time on the most valuable business building opportunities and not on the items that you can delegate for less.

And, for anyone, this dollar-per-hour or "time value" is a great reminder if we think about Tim Ferriss' example of browsing on Amazon to save a few dollars. Whenever you feel yourself pulled into something and you aren't feeling joy from it, then remind yourself what the value of your time is– and readjust yourself into an activity that is a better use of your time.

Transitioning from Hourly to Project or Retainer

Hourly billing is a tricky beast for service-based business owners, because as soon as you become more experienced and efficient, you earn less. Why should you take a penalty for becoming faster at your work?

Many service-based businesses work themself into a problem because they charge an hourly rate, but then don't increase it as they become more efficient. That leaves little room to increase your income. Your clients should be paying for the end result or the transformation, and honestly quicker (as long as it's not rushed and full of mistakes) would be better. I'd rather not pay per hour for the amount of hours the transformation takes.

For example, if I am buying a ticket to travel from Pennsylvania to California I would expect it to cost more for a plane ticket than a train ticket. The plane gets me there faster. And if I could step into a portal in Pennsylvania and instantly step out the other side in California, I would expect that to cost much more than the plane ticket. Because the end result is what matters most.

Pricing by the project or on a monthly retainer basis allows you as an expert to make the amount that you deserve without having to submit a listing of hours spent each month.

To do this, I would take a high estimate of the amount of time I'd expect the work to take. Then, I'd multiply it by my dollar-per-hour. And then I'd have the total project price. This can be broken into phases or charged by milestones achieved, but it's an easy way to ensure you are stepping into your true value.

I have a friend who's client was recently interviewing an executive coach for his team. One coach who they talked to about the project gave them a proposal of $1.2M for the year. He didn't have a team- it was just him. He was literally selling his time. And instead of pricing himself like an employee, or by the hour, he went ahead and was living in his true value.

The Head Summary

1. Step into your true value by doing activities that you enjoy and get you in your flow.

2. Calculate your desired dollar-per-hour (or time value) to help easily decide on your service prices and what items should be delegated.

3. More time should not equal more money. More value should equal more money.

The Head Reflection

What activities are you doing which are below your ideal dollar-per-hour/ time-value? How can you plan to delegate those activities?

How comfortable are you with your ideal dollar-per-hour? Does it feel like an amount you are comfortable owning for yourself? What are some ways you can shift your identity into owning this time-value for yourself?

Wrap Up

This text came out of a compilation of my experiences with the clients I mentioned, as well as continual conversations with people who were trying to find their "next thing".

I have this endless supply of ideas and value to step into. Because I've seen and realized that money can literally come out of my mind. I can think something, speak it into existence, and be paid for it. So can anyone.

But at the end of the day, none of us can want something for someone more than they want it for themselves.

That means, you can't constantly seek help hoping someone will save you. Remember, everything you need exists within yourself. It simply has to be accessed.

It also means that once you make this magic work for yourself, you may feel compelled to help others with this information. But not everyone is ready for it. Some may resent you. Others may think it wouldn't work for them. Everyone needs to have their own time and place to realize they have the inner power.

If after reading this, you are still feeling stuck-- then pick and try just one thing from this book. Choose your favorite section and begin thinking about the world in that way. And revisit and re-read the book again, in a few weeks, to see if you can absorb and believe anything new. You will be in a new place in your personal journey, and ready for another challenge to step into.

Resources and Inspiration

The following books, authors, entrepreneurs, and thought leaders have inspired me in my thoughts and writing.

The Alchemist by Paulo Coelho
The Secret by Rhonda Byrne
The Wisdom of the Enneagram by Don Richard Riso
The Quantum Leap Strategy by Price Pritchett
You 2: A High Velocity Formula for Multiplying Your Personal Effectiveness in Quantum Leaps by Price Pritchett
The Big Leap by Gay Hendricks
Get Rich Lucky Bitch by Denise Duffield- Thomas
The Science of Getting Rich by Wallace D Wattles
Secrets of the Millionaire Mind by Harv Eker
You are a Badass at Making Money by Jen Sincero
You Were Born Rich by Bob Proctor
The Illusion of Money by Kyle Cease
Rich As F*ck by Amanda Frances
Dollars Flow to Me Easily by Richard Dotts
The Trick to Money is Having Some by Stuart Wilde
We Should All Be Millionaires by Rachel Adams
Becoming Supernatural by Dr. Joe Dispenza
Psycho-Cybernetics by Maxwell Maltz
The Inner Game of Tennis by W. Timothy Gallwey
The 4-Hour Workweek by Timothy Ferriss

Emily Wilcox (@em.makes.money)
Xtina Harmsworth (@xtina_harmsworth_empire)
Denise Duffield-Thomas (@denisedt)

Thoughts and Acknowledgements

I started writing this book in 2019 (and now am publishing it in 2023), and although there were many times I thought I was "ready" to publish, that tricky concept of stepping into my own value would get it in the way.

After committing and re-committing to myself multiple times that I can actually publish a book on this topic, I finally decided it was time to let myself be pulled towards the version of me who is a thought leader in this space.

I'd like to acknowledge the 5 people I spend the most time with.

To Rich Quigley, my husband, who goes along with whatever opportunity I want to pursue and always has endless faith in what I can accomplish.

To Kristen Struys, my first employee. The one who keeps all my ideas and projects organized and gently prompts me to keep on going.

To Lauren Williams, my business bestie and confidant on all things. Thank you for being such a big part of my life.

To Emily Wilcox, my long time coach and mentor. Thank you for supporting me to dig deeper and clear space for my transformation.

To myself, for believing so strongly in everything I do, and for knowing myself well enough to trust my intuition and let it guide me.

About Erica

Erica is an entrepreneur, dreamer, philanthropist, and *operational visionary*. She has the gift of being able to see the big picture, and the skill to bring it to life.

She can go from dissecting the technical processes running large companies down to the inner human processes that makes entrepreneurs tick. And that's the theme of structure and process which is weaving the masterpiece she creates.

Her big-picture thinking is also a perfect fit for mentorship and she is passionate about helping business owners through the process of stepping into their value.

Erica enjoys giving back to her community, and is involved in many organizations near and dear to her heart, including Girls on the Run.